The Quigleys Wild Life

SOUTHCOATES PRIMARY SCHOOL
SOUTHCOATES LANE
HULL
HU9 3TW

Written by Simon Mason
Illustrated by Claire Clements

Published by Pearson Education Limited, Edinburgh Gate, Harlow, Essex, CM20 2JE
Registered company number: 872828

www.pearsonschools.co.uk

Text © Simon Mason 2011

Designed by Bigtop

Original illustrations © Pearson Education 2011

Illustrated by Claire Clements

The right of Simon Mason to be identified as author of this work has been asserted by him in accordance with the Copyright, Designs and Patents Act 1988.

First published 2011

15 14 13 12 11
10 9 8 7 6 5 4 3 2 1

British Library Cataloguing in Publication Data
A catalogue record for this book is available from the British Library

ISBN 978 1 408 27382 1

Copyright notice
All rights reserved. No part of this publication may be reproduced in any form or by any means (including photocopying or storing it in any medium by electronic means and whether or not transiently or incidentally to some other use of this publication) without the written permission of the copyright owner, except in accordance with the provisions of the Copyright, Designs and Patents Act 1988 or under the terms of a licence issued by the Copyright Licensing Agency, Saffron House, 6-10 Kirby Street, London EC1N 8TS (www.cla.co.uk). Applications for the copyright owner's written permission should be addressed to the publisher.

Printed and bound in Malaysia (CTP-VVP)

Acknowledgements
We would like to thank the children and teachers of Bangor Central Integrated Primary School, NI; Bishop Henderson C of E Primary School, Somerset; Brookside Community Primary School, Somerset; Cheddington Combined School, Buckinghamshire; Cofton Primary School, Birmingham; Dair House Independent School, Buckinghamshire; Deal Parochial School, Kent; Newbold Riverside Primary School, Rugby and Windmill Primary School, Oxford for their invaluable help in the development and trialling of the Bug Club resources.

Every effort has been made to contact copyright holders of material reproduced in this book. Any omissions will be rectified in subsequent printings if notice is given to the publishers.

Contents

Official Quigley Tour Guide   5

So Many Interesting Facts   10

A Large Shed   21

A Purring Noise   39

Official Quigley Tour Guide

One Saturday morning the Quigleys drove to a wildlife park. They were all excited, especially Will. Mum was looking forward to the gardens, Dad was looking forward to the café and Lucy was looking forward to the children's farmyard with its lop-eared rabbits and pot-bellied piglets and soft yellow chicks.

But Will, who loved big animals best, was looking forward to the rhinos, lions and jaguars.

Will knew a lot about animals. It was incredible how much he knew. In the car he did a quiz, so the others could enjoy how much he knew.

"How many times a week does a two-toed sloth poo?"

No one knew the answer.

"Once," Will said, correctly. "Five points to me. Why do meerkats have black patches round their eyes?"

No one knew that either.

"To help them see in the sun. Like wearing sunglasses. Five points to me and a bonus point for knowing how to spell meerkat."

"What does the Brazilian tapir use its upper lip for?"

No one knew, especially not Lucy. Mum smiled at her sympathetically.

"Come on, Lucy," Will said.

"I don't know," she said crossly, "and I don't care, and neither does Mum."

But Mum and Dad were so proud of Will knowing so much that they agreed to him being Official Quigley Tour Guide when they got to the park.

So Many Interesting Facts

It was a large wildlife park in the middle of the countryside. There was a hothouse full of steam and large, lazy fish, a reptile house where nothing ever moved but sat very still watching with unblinking eyes, and a bat house, horribly dark and full of swooping shadows.

There were animals of every sort – from small, silky ones like guinea pigs to large, fierce ones like leopards.

Will became extremely excited. First, he took the Quigleys to see the massive Southern White Rhinos grazing quietly behind their ditch.

Then he took them to see the large-jawed Nile crocodiles in the reptile house.

Then to the bat house, where the vampires lived.

Everywhere they went, Will told them interesting facts. Occasionally, he continued with his quiz. "How many animals do you know beginning with the letter 'q'? I know quail, queen bee, and … quick-step robber frog. That's another fifteen points to me. I'm on a hundred and thirty-two. How many are you on, Lucy?"

After the bat house, Will wanted to go straight to the lion enclosure, but Dad asked him to slow down. Also to calm down.

"You're too excitable, Will. Ask Lucy what she wants to do."

"All right. What do you want to see next, Lucy? How about the lions? Or the jaguars?"

"I want to see the farmyard."

"But the farmyard's full of boring, little animals. Who wants to see boring, little animals?"

"I do," Lucy said. "There's nothing wrong with that."

Will frowned and consulted his map. "The best way to the farmyard," he said, cunningly, "is past the lion enclosure."

Going past the lion enclosure, they paused for about twenty minutes while Will told them interesting facts about lions.

" ... and their roar can be heard up to six miles away," he said, which seemed true because as he was talking a lion roared and it had the effect of flinging him behind a nearby bush. Although he said he liked big, fierce animals, Will was more nervous of them than he cared to admit.

"Farmyard now!" Lucy cried.

"Which is just past the jaguars," Will said.

It turned out that the farmyard was also just past the Arabian leopards and the Canadian timber wolves, about which Will knew a lot of other interesting facts.

"Leopards can crunch through a skull in a single bite," he told the Quigleys. "And wolves like to rip out throats. You see, Lucy, they all have their own special way of killing."

"They all have their own special smell too," Lucy said. She had noticed this earlier. Some smells (like the bats' smell) made you cough, some (like the flamingos') made your eyes run, and some (like the rhinos') were so bad that you had to walk on tiptoe, with your face pointing up at the sky, or you would fall unconscious to the ground.

"But when are we going to the *farmyard*?" she demanded.

Will ignored her. With great relish, he related many more fascinating facts about ripping, biting, tearing, chewing and crunching, and Mum was so fascinated she said she had to go and sit down in the café.

Dad offered to help her sit down. He also said it would be nice, while they were sitting down in the café, if Will took Lucy to the farmyard. Not past the bone-crushing boa constrictors or the vicious hyenas. But *directly* to the farmyard. In silence, if possible.

Will sighed. "All right," he said.

A Large Shed

Will and Lucy walked along the path together.

"First I'm going to see the chicks," Lucy said, "and then I'm going to see the rabbits. You like rabbits, don't you, Will? They're very soft."

"No," Will said. "I like fierce things. *I'm* fierce."

"No, you're not, Will. I've seen you stroke rabbits. Your face goes all smiley and you make that purring noise."

"I do not," Will said indignantly. "You're mixing me up with someone else. I like animals that bite and roar and trample their prey into the mud."

Lucy thought about this.

"I know you don't," she said.

"Right then," Will said hotly. "Let's play predators and we'll see if I like it. I'll be a slavering, slobbering grizzly bear and you can be ... a small girl lost in the woods."

He stuck out his arms and hunched his shoulders and made his eyes small and greedy until he looked nothing at all like a bear, and began to growl.

"Don't, Will," Lucy said, calmly. "You'll hurt yourself."

He lunged at her a bit to see what she would do.

"If you don't stop," Lucy said, "I'll go to the farmyard on my own."

Will didn't stop, so Lucy turned down a different path and marched across a small bridge. Then (because Will was still lumbering around her in an unbear-like way), she climbed through a wooden fence, ran across a grass verge and fell into a ditch.

The ditch was a surprise, and Lucy lay there for a while. Luckily, it was a grassy ditch, quite soft, and she wasn't hurt. She got up and climbed out. Will was still on the other side of the fence, saying something quite fast, but she ignored him, and set off in the opposite direction across a field towards a low, brick building. Will shouted after her, but she carried on ignoring him.

It was a nice, peaceful field, very large and empty. As Lucy walked, she thought happily about the farmyard. There would be guinea pigs to stroke, and lambs to bottle-feed, and – best of all – chicks so soft it would be like holding little puffs of warm air. She smiled to herself. She didn't like big, fierce things; she liked small, cuddly things. There was nothing wrong with that.

Soon she came to a part of the field which was all churned up, as if something very big had been walking about there.

Then she noticed the smell. She had smelled it before; it was the smell that made her walk on tiptoe, looking up at the sky. It was a pity Will wasn't there to remind her which animal it came from.

As Lucy walked on, she wondered vaguely where Will was.

At last, she stopped tiptoeing, and lowered her face and looked about – and there was Will, on the other side of the fence that was attached to the building in front of her. He must have run along the path to get there. He still seemed to be doing his bear impression. But after a moment she realised he was pointing to the doorway of the building.

Even odder, he was putting his finger to his lips and making wild get-out-of-the-way gestures.

"Go away, Will," Lucy said.

As she spoke, she peered into the building.

"By the way," she added. "Which smell is this? I know it's one of the bad ones."

Through the doorway, in the shadows, she saw the outline of something. Something big.

At first she thought it was a bulldozer. Or a large shed.

Then it moved, and she realised it was an animal. An animal twenty times bigger than her.

From his side of the fence,
Will watched in horror as
the Southern White Rhino
slowly emerged
from its house.
It took a long
time because
it was so big.

Some interesting
facts came into
Will's mind,
such as: Rhinos
have a terrible
temper.

Their eyesight is
poor but their sense
of smell is good.
They display
aggression by
panting and
wiping their large front
horn on the ground.

The rhino
panted and
wiped its large
front horn on
the ground.

Other facts went through Will's mind, such as: Mum and Dad are in the café. Lucy is in danger. I am in big trouble.

Looking at the panting rhino, he didn't feel so keen on large, fierce animals anymore.

Then, without thinking anything else, he climbed over the fence, scrambled down into the ditch and up the other side and stood in front of the rhino, about twenty yards away.

Immediately, it turned its great horned head towards him.

Will stood very still, facing it. "Lucy," he whispered out of the corner of his mouth. "Don't make any noise. Just start to walk, very quietly, very slowly, to the fence. I'll distract it."

As Lucy began to move, the rhino turned its head back towards her, but before it could do anything else, Will began to talk to it, not in his usual excitable voice, but very, *very* calmly.

"Hello, Mr Ceratotherium Simum Simum," he said, quietly. This was the Southern White Rhino's Latin name. "I just wanted to say ... how much I like rhinos. I like your two horns, and I like your three toes on each of your four feet, and I like the way you have hair in your ears. It's pretty good hair. And they're pretty good ears."

The rhino waggled its ears in Will's direction and Will heard Lucy climbing over the fence behind him.

He tried to think of something else to say.

"I like black rhinos," he said, in the same lulling voice as before, "and I like Indian rhinos and Javan rhinos, and I even like Sumatran rhinos. But I like white rhinos best, and I always have. It's true. I wouldn't lie to you."

The rhino looked at Will, and Will looked at the rhino, and the rhino seemed so very big that Will didn't know what to say anymore. "Well. Thank you," he said after a moment. "I'm going to go now." Slowly and quietly, he backed away to the fence, and, slowly and quietly, climbed over it to where Lucy was waiting, and as soon as he reached her, his legs stopped working and he fell onto the ground.

A Purring Noise

After various explanations, made first to some people who came running up to them, and then to a rather shouty keeper, and lastly to Mum and Dad, Will and Lucy went to the children's farmyard.

Will was being very quiet.

Although they had been cross, Mum and Dad began to feel sorry for him.

"Is there anything else you want to see before we go, Will?"

He shook his head.

"Any man-eating wart-leopards or throat-ripping hyena pigs?"

"No, thank you."

He went to sit with Lucy in the handling pen with the rabbits and the guinea pigs and the soft yellow chicks. Lucy passed them one by one to Will, and he stroked them, and after a while he stopped being quiet and pale and his face went smiley, and he began to make a purring noise.

"Told you," Lucy said.

Will gave her a look. "There's nothing wrong with that," he said.